ABC's
of
the Coral Reef

George J Robinson Ph.D.

Published by: EnviroScribes
Mahopac, New York

ISBN-10: **1508655375**
ISBN-13: **978-1508655374**

Other Books by Dr. Robinson

Bird Banding

The ABC Guide to the Everglades

Naturebooksbygeorge.com

Dear Reader:

Try to guess what coral reef creature is about to appear from the pictured hints. Good Luck!

Aa is for …… (Hint)

Aa is for **Angel** Fish

An angel fish's thin, flexible body can twist through narrow spaces in the reef.

Bb is for ......

Bb is for **Butterfly** Fish

The extra eye on the rear of the butterfly fish confuses predators.

Cc is for ......

Cc is for **Clown** Fish

Clown fish like to towel in anemones.

Dd is for ......

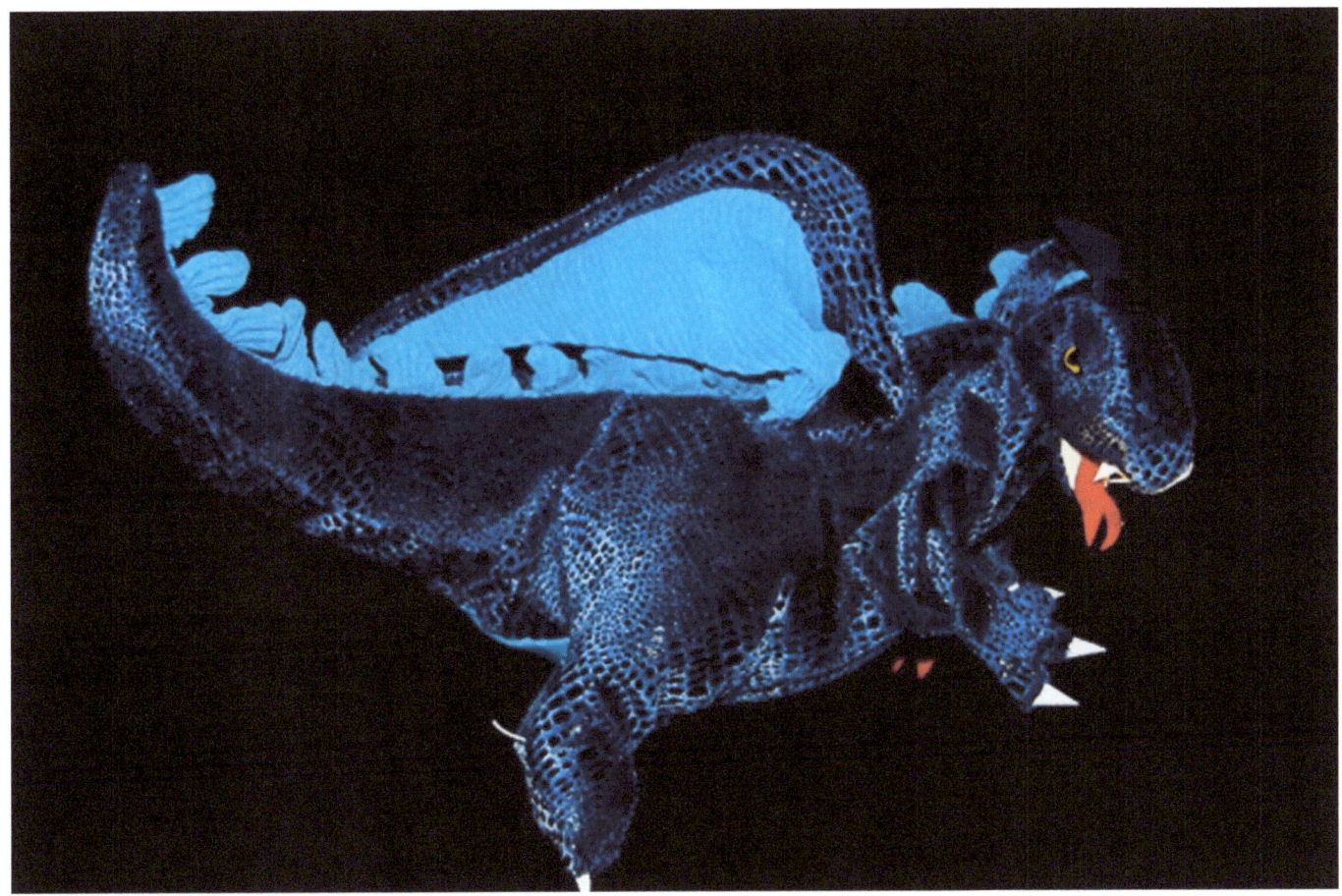

Dd is for **Dragon** Seahorse

The weedy dragon seahorse is easily camouflaged in the reef's seascape.

Ee is for ......

Ee is for **Eagle** Ray

Eagle rays glide through the sea like their namesakes through the sky.

Ff is for ......

Ff is for **Frog** Fish

Frog fish lull their prey into thinking they are part of the reef. Then BAM! They attack.

Gg is for ......

Gg is for **Goat** Fish

Goat fish use their long chin barbels
to probe the seafloor for food.

Hh is for ......

Hh is for **Hog** Fish

The hog fish gets its name from its elongated pig-like snout and rooting behavior.

Ii is for ......

Ii is for **Irish** Lord

The red Irish lord is very common
in Alaskan waters.

Jj is for ......

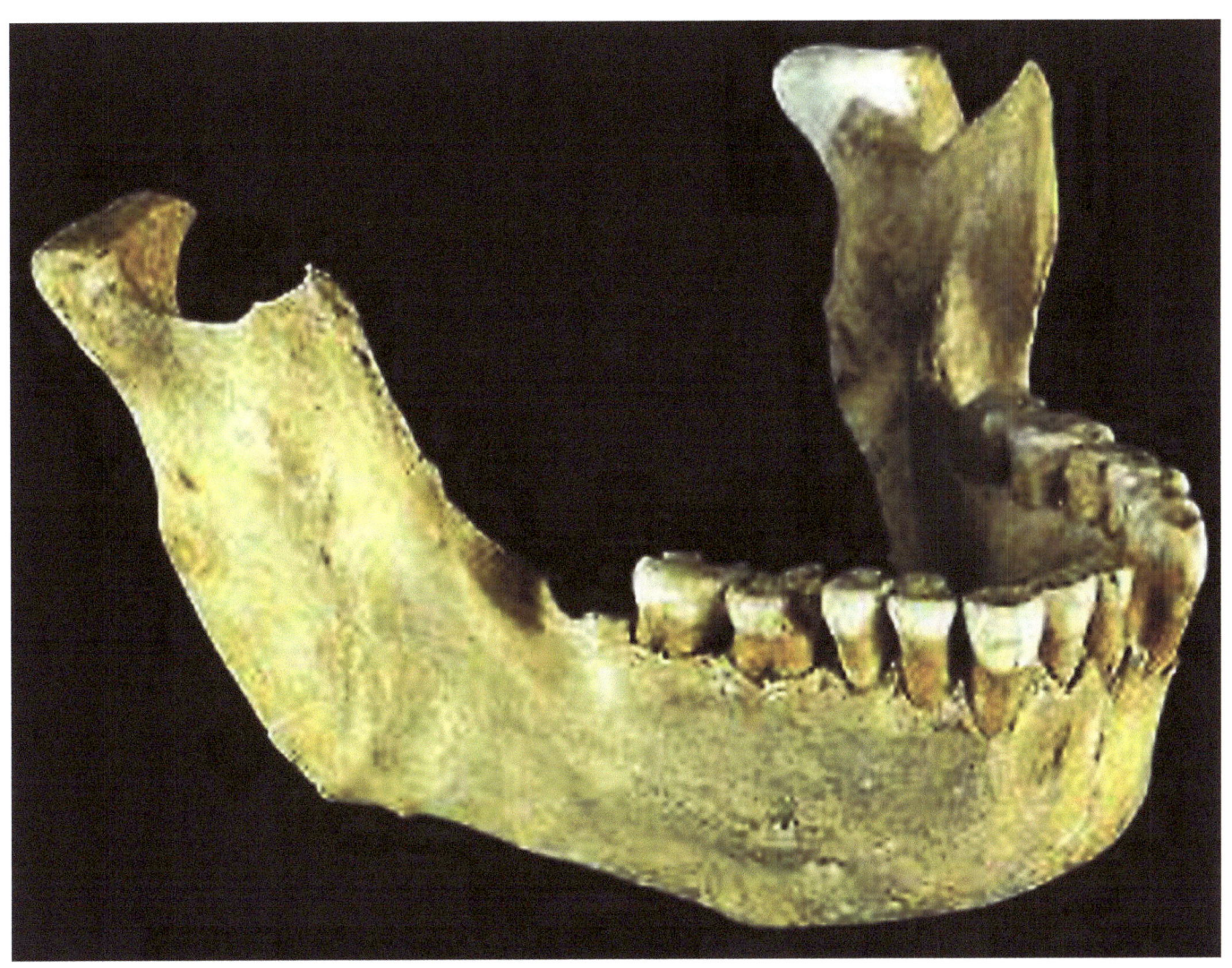

Jj is for **Jaw** fish

The jaw fish incubates its young in its mouth.

Kk is for ......

Kk is for **King** Angel Fish

Juvenile king fish act as cleaner fish for hammer head sharks and manta rays.

Ll is for ......

Ll is for **Lion** Fish

The lion fish is very toxic if you touch it.

Mm is for ......

Mm is for **Moon** Jellyfish

A moon jelly's sting is not painful unlike other jelly fish.

Nn is for ......

Nn is for **Nurse** Shark

A nurse shark is not considered dangerous under normal circumstances.

Oo is for ......

Oo is for **Orange** Sea Cucumber

This creature has 10 tentacles
which it uses to feed itself.

Pp is for ......

Pp is for **Parrot** Fish

A parrot fish nibbles on the coral and so can poop a ton of sand a year.

Qq is for ......

Qq is for **Queen** Angel Fish

A queen angel fish is recognized
by the crown on her head.

Rr is for ......

Rr is for **Rabbit** Fish

Male rabbit fish have claspers on their underside making them look like "fish with legs".

Ss is for ......

Ss is for **Scorpion** Fish

A scorpion fish's spines are venomous.

Tt is for ......

Tt is for Sand **Tiger** Shark

Sand tiger sharks have a mouth full of teeth that protrude in all directions.
Yet, they are not aggressive.

Uu is for ......

Uu is for **Unicorn** fish.

When unicorn fish fight, they don't use their horns; but rather, they use the razors on their tails.

Vv is for ......

Vv is for **Vase** Sponge

The velvet vase sponge is not a plant.
It belongs to the animal kingdom.

Ww is for ......

Ww is for **Wolf** Eel

Male and female wolf eels pair for life.

Xx is for ......

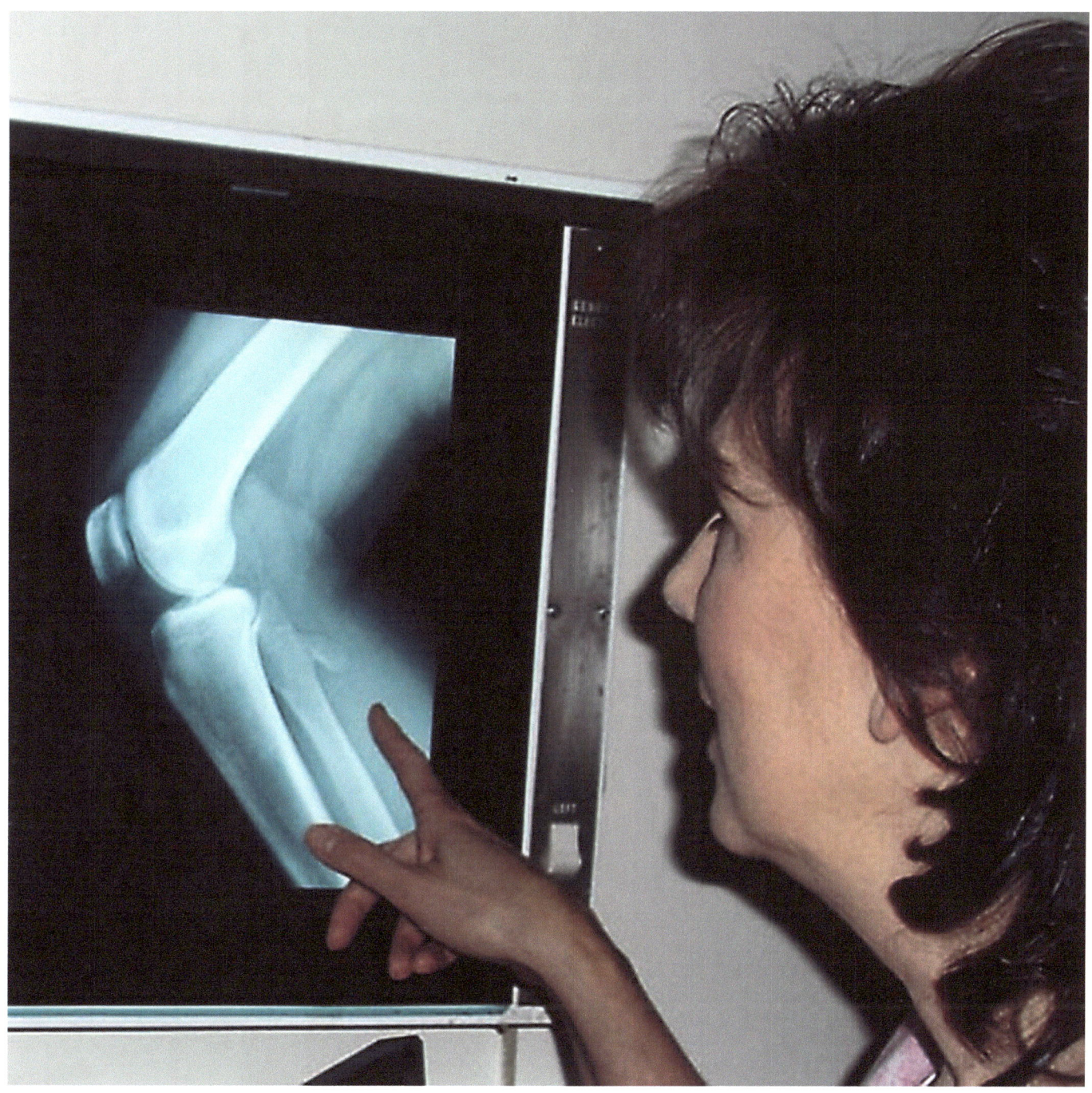

Xx is for **X-Ray** Fish

X-ray fish live in coastal waters near coral reefs. Scientist use them for research on pollution.

Yy is for ......

Yy is for **Yellow** Tail Snapper

Yellow tail snappers feed on shrimp, crabs, worms and smaller fish.

Zz is for ......

Zz is for **Zebra** Shark

Zebra sharks are nocturnal and spend most of their time resting on the sea floor during the day.
Photo Credit: The Atlanta Aquarium